DECODABLE BOOK 3

Orlando   Boston   Dallas   Chicago   San Diego

Visit *The Learning Site!*

www.harcourtschool.com

D0166894

Printed in the United States of America

ISBN 0-15-326683-X

14   179   10 09 08 07

Ordering Options
ISBN 0-15-323767-8 (Collection)
ISBN 0-15-326717-8 (package of 5)

Contents

Z/17

Sid

by Susan Blackaby   illustrated by Nathan Jarvis

Look at what Sid did.
Liz is mad at Sid.

Sid ran and hid. Zip!

Did Dad see Sid?

Did Tim see him?

Did Tip see him?

Is Sid here?

It is Sid!

Sid has a gift for Liz.

Tim and Pip

by Lisa deMauro

illustrated by Ande Cook

Tim and Pip are pals.

Tim sits on a mat.
Tim will have a nap.

Will Pip nap?

Pip sits in a big hat.

Tim has his nap.

Will Pip nap?

Pip naps on Tim!

Sid

Word Count: 40

High-Frequency Words

for
here
look
see
what

Decodable Words*

a
and
at
Dad
did
gift
has
hid
him
is
it
Liz
mad
ran
Sid
Tim
Tip
zip

*Words with /i/ *i* appear in **boldface** type.

Tim and Pip

Word Count: 38

High-Frequency Words

are
have
on

Decodable Words

a
and
big
has
hat
his
in
mat
nap
naps
pals
Pip
sits
Tim
will

*Words with /i/ appear in **boldface** type.